# THE
# JAPANESE

Clare Doran

**Thomson Learning**
**New York**

## Look into the Past

**The Ancient Chinese**
**The Anglo-Saxons**
**The Aztecs**
**The Egyptians**
**The Greeks**
**The Incas**
**The Japanese**
**The Maya**
**The Normans**
**The Romans**
**The Sioux**
**The Vikings**

First published in the
United States in 1995 by
Thomson Learning
115 Fifth Avenue
New York, NY 10003

First published in 1994 by Wayland (Publishers) Ltd.

U.K. version copyright © 1994 Wayland (Publishers) Ltd.

U.S. version copyright © 1995 Thomson Learning

Library of Congress Cataloging-in-Publication Data
Doran, Clare.
  The Japanese / Clare Doran.
        p.       cm. — (Look into the past)
  Includes bibliographical references and index.
  ISBN 1-56847-173-4
  1. Japan — History — Tokugawa period, 1600–1868 —
Pictorial works — Juvenile literature. [1. Japan — History
— Tokugawa period, 1600-1868. 2. Tokyo (Japan) —
History.] I. Title. II. Series.
DS871.D67      1995
952'.025 — dc20                              94-32456

Printed in Italy

**Picture acknowledgments**
The publishers would like to thank the following for
supplying the pictures in this book: Ancient Art and
Architecture Collection 8, 15 (both), 17 (top), 23 (bottom),
25 (both), 28; Chapel Studios 29 (top); E. T. Archive 17
(bottom, Victoria & Albert Museum), 27 (bottom right);
Edo-Tokyo Museum 11 (bottom), 14, 20, 24 (left); Robert
Harding 10 (Nigel Blythe), 18 (right), 21 (bottom), 22;
Suzanne Perrin 5 (bottom); Shin`enKan Foundation 21
(top); Tokyo National Museum 11 (top), 13 (top), 16, 27
(top right); Wayland Picture Library 12; Werner Forman
Archive 5 (top, Kuroda Collection), 6, 9 (both, L J
Anderson Collection), 13 (bottom, Kita-In, Saitumi), 18
(left), 26 (Kita-In, Saitumi).
Map artwork on page 4 by Jenny Hughes.

# CONTENTS

Words that appear in **bold italic** in the text are explained in the glossary on page 30.

# THE BIRTH OF A CITY

Japan is a country that is made up of four main islands and many smaller islands. They lie in the Pacific Ocean, to the east of China. Japan has gone through many changes throughout its history. We are going to look at a famous period when the city of Edo became Japan's capital in the seventeenth century. This was the time of *samurai* warriors and leaders called *shoguns*.

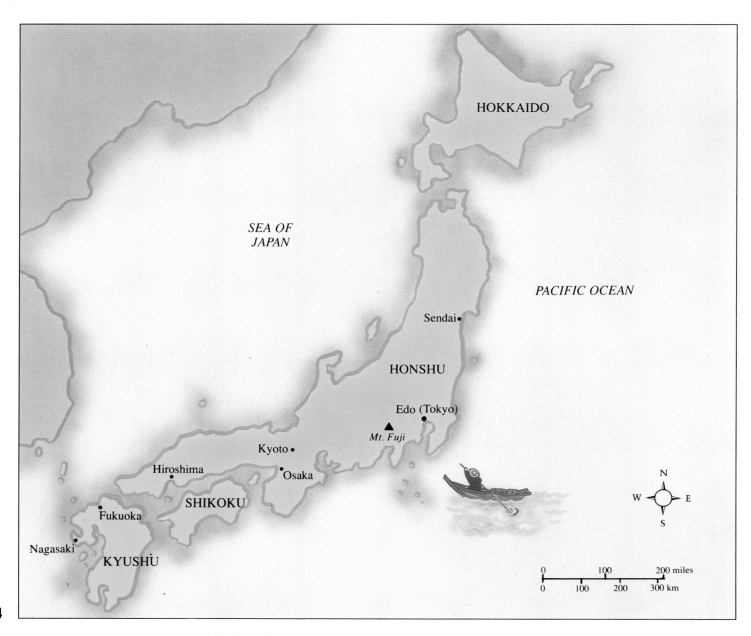

HOKKAIDO

*SEA OF JAPAN*

*PACIFIC OCEAN*

Sendai•

HONSHU

Edo (Tokyo)•

▲ *Mt. Fuji*

Kyoto •

Hiroshima •       • Osaka

SHIKOKU

• Fukuoka

Nagasaki •

KYUSHU

N
W — E
S

| 0 | 100 | 200 miles |
| 0 | 100 | 200 | 300 km |

Before 1603 the different provinces of Japan had been fighting one another for hundreds of years. Peace finally came to Japan in 1603, as did one common ruler – Tokugawa Ieyasu. To reward Ieyasu for ending the centuries of war, the emperor of Japan gave him the title "shogun." This title means "commander-in-chief for beating the barbarians." The shogun made Edo his home. This village eventually grew into one of the largest and liveliest cities in the world at that time. Many years later the name of this city changed to Tokyo, the present capital of Japan.

Tokugawa Ieyasu ▶ not only helped to set up the city of Edo, but he also started a new period of Japanese history, when shoguns ruled and the emperor was only a symbol. This stretch of history lasted for 250 years and is called the Edo period or the Tokugawa period.

5

# EDO CITY

Ieyasu brought his loyal lords to Edo, but it took many years to change the muddy fishing village into a powerful city. Roads had to be built and marshes filled so that the land could be used. Bridges were built over the many rivers, and canals were dug so that food and other materials could be transported easily. The biggest danger to Edo was fire. Fires would often start after earthquakes. In fact, fires were so common they were called the "flowers of Edo." They often destroyed large areas of the city.

Edo Castle become a sign of the power and strength of the shogun. Over a number of years, the castle grew larger and grander. When the castle was finished, it had 66 gates and 36 guard posts.

▲ Inside the grounds were bridges, ponds, and stables. This picture of Nijo Castle in Kyoto, the old capital of Japan, shows us what a Japanese castle looks like. Notice the wide moat and decorated roof tiles.

This bridge, called Nihonbashi, was the center of Edo city and was called the "bridge of Japan." The five main roads that spread through Japan started from this bridge. All kinds of people, from the very rich to the very poor, crossed over Nihonbashi.

This is a map of Edo city. Notice the boats coming in at the bottom left. Waterways were very important for transporting people and goods throughout Japan.

Since the northeast was thought to be an unlucky direction, *temples* were built in the northeast to protect the city from bad luck that might come from there.

7

# THE PEOPLE OF EDO

**People were divided into four main groups, depending on their family background and the type of work they did. This class system had originally come from China as part of a way of thinking called *Confucianism*. The four main classes in order of importance were the warrior class, also known as the samurai; the farmers; the craftsmen; and the merchants.**

The samurai were seen as the top of society and were supposed to set a good example to the ordinary people. Only samurai were allowed to wear two swords. In this painting, each samurai is wearing a long sword and a short sword. Samurai also had a special hairstyle. They shaved the fronts of their heads and tied the rest of the hair into a ponytail that was doubled over.

The smaller piece of armor shown here was made to give to a boy when he reached the age of 14. At this time his hair would also be dressed in an adult style. The samurai armor had a breastplate to protect the chest and pieces to protect the legs, arms, and neck. The design of the helmet was important. It might be in the shape of an animal. A samurai believed the helmet would help him look frightening and would scare the enemy. ▼

▲ This close-up shows how bright pieces of cord were placed over the iron of the armor. The sleeves were based on armor owned by a famous Japanese warrior named Minamoto Yoshitsune.

# THE FARMERS

The largest group of people in Edo Japan were the farmers. The farmers were seen as very important because they grew the country's rice. In fact, rice was so precious that some people's wealth was decided not by how much money they had, but by how much rice their land could grow. However, the farmers' lives were very hard. They worked outside all day, and even the evenings brought no time to relax. They were busy making sacks and ropes out of straw. There were times when there was little food to eat, and bad weather made their job very difficult.

Growing rice took a lot of time and involved every member of the family. The fields were flooded with water for the young rice plants to grow. The members of the family worked together – planting, watering, weeding, and harvesting the rice. It is still grown in the same way today.

▲ During the cold weather a farmer wore a cloak made of straw and a hat made of bamboo. His sandals were also made of straw, and pieces of cloth were tied around his legs and lower arms for extra warmth.

Farmers' houses varied a lot from region to region. Often the roofs were made of thatch and were low so that snow would easily fall off them. For warmth, the family sat around the fire, which they also used for cooking.

# THE CRAFTSMEN

As more people moved from the countryside and came to live in the city of Edo, the job of the craftsmen became more important. Many new buildings were needed, and the skills of the craftsmen were in demand. Craftsmen learned their trade by starting out as *apprentices*. When they were very young, they left their families to live with a master who would teach them his skill. If he was lucky, the apprentice would take over the master's business when the master grew old.

Townspeople lived in small, narrow houses. They went to public baths every day to bathe. They also met their friends there and caught up on the local gossip.

The people in this picture are sword grinders. Their job was to keep the swords of the samurai sharp. People believed swords had a special power, and it was important to take good care of them. These sword grinders are sharpening a sword, and the man at the bottom of the picture is bringing them more swords in a box. ▼

◄ There were a variety of types of craftsmen in Edo. Many craftsmen, such as plasterers, carpenters, roofers, or stonemasons, were involved in the making of buildings. Artist Katsushika Hokusai drew craftsmen, capturing the movement of their bodies as they lifted and strained.

▲ Here is a young boy selling fresh cold water in the streets. He wears a straw hat to protect his head from the sun.

# THE MERCHANTS

According to the government, the merchants had the lowest position in Edo society. This was because they did not produce useful products such as swords or rice, but earned their living by selling other people's work. Still, merchants played a very important role, setting up shops, helping trade grow, lending money to the samurai, and growing rich themselves. The government tried to pass laws that would stop the merchants from showing off their new wealth. For example, they were not supposed to wear expensive silk clothes. But merchants often broke this law by lining the inside of their clothes with brightly colored silk.

The Mitsui family was a powerful merchant family. By 1700 their shop, called Echigoya, had become Japan's largest store. They introduced the idea of selling goods at a definite price, rather than deciding with each customer what the price should be. They also sold material cut to the size that the customer wanted, rather than selling only one large piece of material.

There were many different types of money in Edo. Gold, silver, copper, and iron coins were used. This large gold coin is called an Oban and was used only on very special occasions. ▼

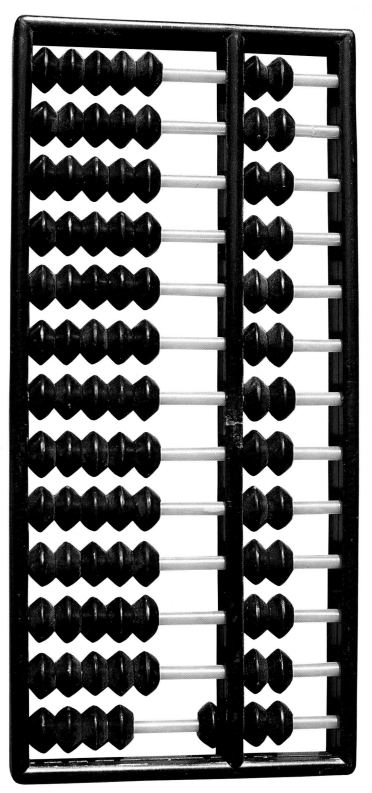

◄ In shops, the usual way of figuring out a bill was by using a beaded instrument called an **abacus**. Not only was the shopkeeper able to add up numbers with the beads, but he could also subtract, multiply, and divide very quickly.

# TRANSPORTATION AND TRAVEL

**The Edo period was a time when travel became possible for more people. People traveled for business as well as for pleasure. A number of roads linked the city of Edo with other towns and cities. The most famous road was called the Tokaido. However, people were not allowed to travel completely freely. At special gates across parts of the road travelers were checked to make sure they had the proper papers that granted them permission to travel.**

◄ As more people traveled for business and pleasure, there needed to be more places for them to rest and eat along the way. Travelers could stop, rest, and be entertained for the evening at various *teahouses* and inns that appeared on roadsides. Sometimes they would spend all their money before they reached the end of their journey.

There are many ► mountains in Japan, so transportation by road was very difficult. The main way of moving goods was by sea. Thousands of boats crossed the water between the large cities of Osaka and Edo.

16

◄ Ferryboats were used to help people cross rivers. When there were no boats, people sat on the shoulders of **porters** who carried them across the river.

# THE THEATER

**Several types of theater thrived in Japan at this time. Among the samurai, a type of drama called *No* was popular. This was mostly slow-moving and serious, with a religious feel about it. For the lower classes, *Kabuki* was an exciting and popular form of entertainment. The leading Kabuki actors were famous throughout the whole country, and books were written about them, praising their handsome appearance and acting skills. Another important form of drama was called *Bunraku*. In Bunraku, puppets were used to act out the story while singers and musicians provided music and songs.**

Colorful makeup and ornate, eye-catching costumes were worn by Kabuki actors. The plays were full of action, with the entrances and exits of the actors onstage being particularly exciting. The audience would shout out its comments even during the performance. Going to the Kabuki theater was an important day out, with plays lasting all day and people eating, drinking, and enjoying one another's company.

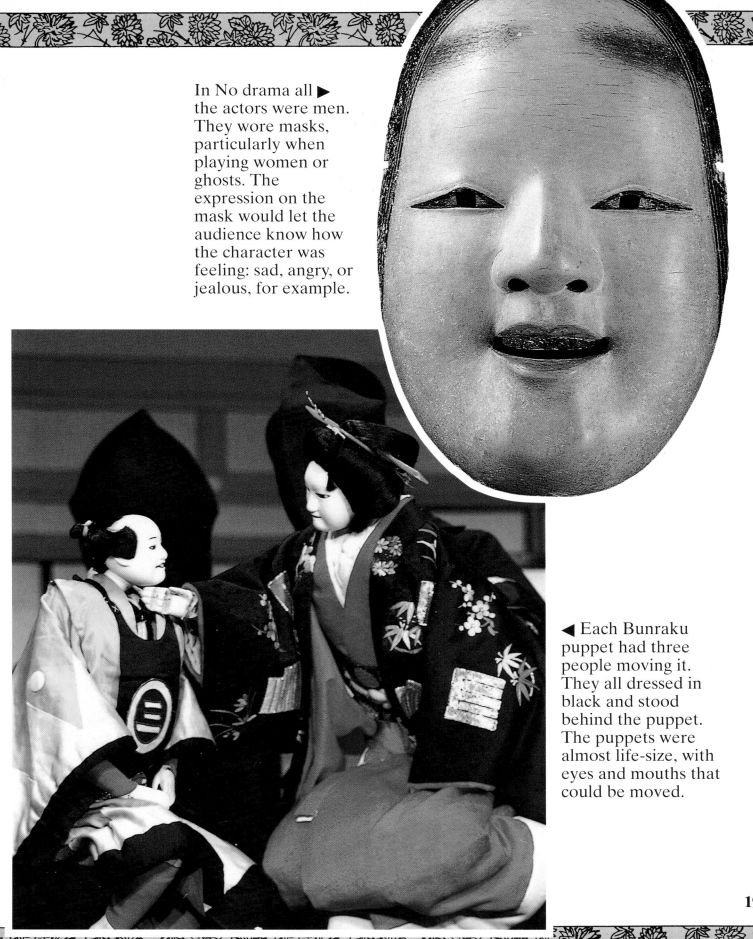

In No drama all ▶ the actors were men. They wore masks, particularly when playing women or ghosts. The expression on the mask would let the audience know how the character was feeling: sad, angry, or jealous, for example.

◀ Each Bunraku puppet had three people moving it. They all dressed in black and stood behind the puppet. The puppets were almost life-size, with eyes and mouths that could be moved.

# THE PLEASURE QUARTERS

Although the government of Edo wanted people to work hard, there were also places where people could escape from work and enjoy themselves. One popular place was the Yoshiwara, where mostly men went to eat, drink, gamble, and relax. It was a long way from the center of Edo, and part of the trip was by boat. Samurai were not supposed to go there, but they often hid their heads under large hats and sneaked in. At night the Yoshiwara was completely closed up. If a careless visitor had not left in time, he had to stay until morning. Once inside the Yoshiwara, it was so different from ordinary life, it was called "the floating world."

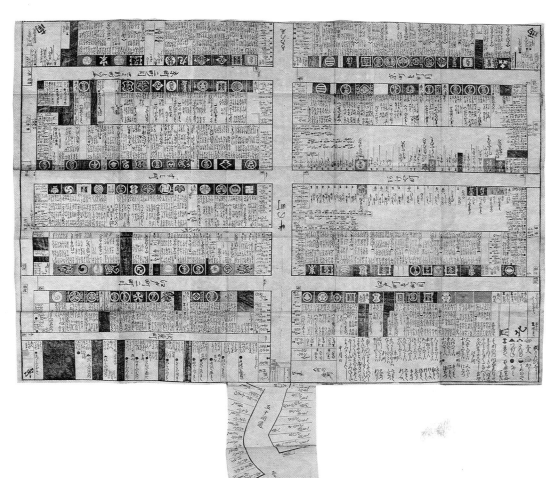

This map shows the layout of the huge area of the Yoshiwara.

As well as having places to eat, drink, and gamble, the Yoshiwara was famous for its entertainment. There were many different types of entertainers, both male and female, but the most popular of these were called **geisha.** The geisha were a special group of women who had been taught from a young age how to dance, sing, and even speak in an elegant fashion.

The way geisha ▶ looked and dressed was very important. They covered their faces in white powder and wore heavy wigs. Their platform shoes were sometimes so high, they needed a maid to help them walk!

By contrast, life for most other women was very hard. They received little respect; they were treated like slaves. Sometimes women were so unhappy they would run away. Usually they were caught and quickly brought back.

# RELIGIONS

During the Edo period, Japanese people followed a number of different religions and philosophies. The oldest religion of Japan is called *Shintoism.* Another important religion was *Buddhism*, which came to Japan in the sixth century. Most people observed both religions, visiting both Shinto *shrines* and Buddhist temples.

People worshiped at holy places called shrines, and sometimes they even went to pray at a rock or a mountain that was believed to be sacred.

In the early ►
eighteenth century a
large Buddhist temple
called Todaiji was
repaired and rebuilt.
The main statue,
called the Great
Buddha, is almost
45 feet high. This is
still the largest bronze
statue in the world,
and the building in
which it is kept is
the largest wooden
building in the world.

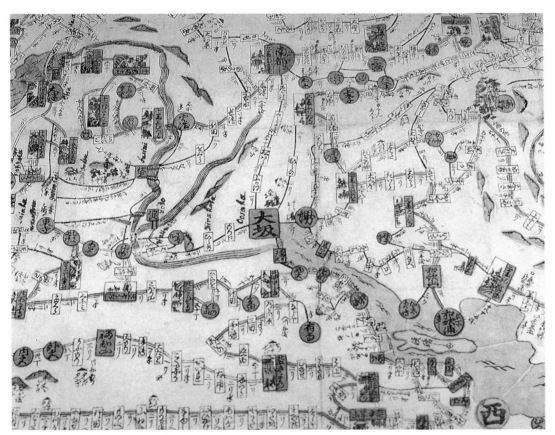

◄ During the Edo
period it became
popular to go on a
***pilgrimage***, both for
religious reasons and
as a good excuse to
travel. Special maps
were used by pilgrims
to visit holy places.
This map shows thirty
places that a pilgrim
could visit to worship
a god called Kannon. **23**

# THE WRITTEN WORD

Most of the citizens of Edo could read, so books were very popular. There were many serious books telling people how to lead good lives or containing facts about law or science. However, people also read books for fun. There were books full of love stories available, as well as books about the great warriors of the past. People could buy books in bookstores or borrow them from libraries.

◄ Books were printed from wooden printing blocks like this. Notice how the shapes of the letters have been carved into the wood. The books could then be printed very cheaply.

Around 1010, Murasaki Shikibu, a woman, completed *The Tale of Genji*. This book has been called the finest piece of Japanese literature and is considered to be the first important novel written in any language.

Wooden blocks like this were also used to make art prints. A print of a famous beautiful woman or, as in this picture, a print of a popular actor could be bought for very little money. ►

# ARTS AND CRAFTS

Japanese people of this time were very interested in the latest fashions, especially those people living in the large cities of Edo, Osaka, and Kyoto. Wealthy citizens spent large amounts of money on expensive clothes. And as the merchants became richer, they also wanted to have beautiful objects in their houses. There were many artists producing beautiful pieces of art and *ceramics*. People were also interested in learning about the arts. Classes in poetry writing, Japanese dance, and the *tea ceremony* became popular.

The *kimono* was a long piece of cloth that ▶ was tied around the body with a wide belt. The design of the kimono material was carefully chosen to suit the age of the wearer and the time of year.

◀ Here is a group of *lacquer* workers. They are carefully preparing wooden boxes and decorating them beautifully.

26

▲ This is a famous writing case designed by the artist Ogata Korin (1658-1716). In the design are a bridge and flowers made of pearl. People of this time knew that Korin was referring to a famous story in Japanese literature. Korin was well known for his pleasing designs and bright use of colors, especially on pottery.

The design of these small boxes, called *inro*, was very important. The boxes were used to carry medicine or other small objects. Some of them were covered in lacquer, which gave them a bright, shiny look.

# THE SEASONS AND FESTIVALS

Several festivals took place during the year. New Year was an especially important holiday season in Edo Japan. People visited friends, relatives, and people with whom they worked. Special foods, such as small cakes made of rice, were eaten. During the summer there was a festival of the dead, when people sang songs and performed dances. Many of the festivals celebrated nature and the seasons, involving rituals such as looking at maple leaves in the autumn.

◄ In spring Japanese people often traveled to see the cherry blossoms. Some places were famous for particularly beautiful blossoms. Huge crowds of people sat under the trees, eating, drinking, and gazing in wonder at the magnificent blossoms.

28

The boys' festival was celebrated on May 5. On this day, a kite in the shape of a carp was flown outside the house. In wealthier households, some armor might be put on display. Here are some carp kites that are flown today to celebrate the boys' festival. ▶

◀ A dolls' festival was celebrated by girls on March 3. Dolls that were meant to look like the emperor and empress of Japan, together with their family and servants, were put on display in the house. Special drinks and sweet cakes were eaten as part of this festival.

29

# GLOSSARY

**Abacus**   A wooden frame with beads that slide up and down for counting.

**Apprentice**   A person who is learning a craft and agrees to stay with his or her teacher as an employee.

**Buddhism**   A religion in which the Buddha, a man who taught how to be free of life's suffering, is honored.

**Bunraku**   Theater in which puppets are used to tell the story.

**Ceramics**   A type of pottery.

**Confucianism**   The ideas of Confucius, a Chinese teacher of morals and human values. In Confucianism, the four major classes are scholar, farmer, craftsman, and merchant.

**Geisha**   A woman who is trained to entertain guests with witty conversation, singing, and dancing.

**Inro**   A small container used to hold medicine or other small objects.

**Kabuki**   Theater based on popular stories. Kabuki is full of exciting acting and attractive costumes.

**Kimono**   A long, loose robe worn with a belt.

**Lacquer**   A hard varnish or finish.

**No**   Theater performed on a plain stage. The performers move in a slow and elegant way.

**Pilgrimage**   A journey to a sacred place.

**Porters**   People employed to carry things.

**Samurai**   The warrior class.

**Shintoism**   Japan's traditional religion that upholds nature as sacred.

**Shogun**   A military leader.

**Shrine**   A place where gods are worshiped.

**Tea ceremony**   A formal occasion when tea is served in a special way.

**Teahouses**   Places where refreshments are served and various kinds of entertainment are available.

**Temples**   Buildings where statues of the Buddha are honored.

# IMPORTANT DATES

**1600** The Tokugawa family begin its rule of Japan. This was to last for the next 250 years.

**1603** Tokugawa Ieyasu brings peace to Japan. He receives the title of shogun from the emperor. Ieyasu makes Edo the new capital of Japan.

**1639** The shogun forbids all contact with the outside world.

**1657** The Great Fire of Meireki burns down large areas of Edo city.

**1675-1725** Genroku period. This time was famous for the growth of culture and the arts.

**1700** Edo is thought to have been the largest city in the world at this time.

**1854** Commodore Matthew Perry lands in Japan. This visit opens up contact between Japan and Western countries.

**1855** Great Edo earthquake.

**1867-68** The last shogun hands over power to the Japanese emperor. The emperor moves to Edo and rules Japan. This is known as the Meiji Restoration.

# BOOKS TO READ

Avakian, Monique. *The Meiji Restoration and the Rise of Moden Japan.* Turning Points in World History. Morristown, NJ: Silver Burdett, 1991.

Kalman, Bobbie. *Japan: The Culture.* New York: Crabtree Publishing Co., 1989.

Leathers, Noel L. *The Japanese in America.* In America Books. Minneapolis: Lerner Publications, 1991.

Lerner Publications Geography Staff. *Japan in Pictures.* Visual Geography Series. Minneapolis: Lerner Publications, 1989.

Odijk, Pamela. *The Japanese.* The Ancient World. Morristown, NJ: Silver Burdett, 1991.

Pilbeam, Mavis. *Japan.* North Pomfret, VT: Trafalgar Square, 1992.

Ridgwell, Jenny. *A Taste of Japan.* Food Around the World. New York: Thomson Learning, 1994.

Steele, A. *A Samurai Warrior.* Vero Beach, FL: Rourke Corp., 1988.

# INDEX